BOOTH AGAIN!

MORE OF GEORGE BOOTH

Andrews and McMeel
A Universal Press Syndicate Company
Kansas City • New York

ISBN: 0-8362-1843-4

Library of Congress Catalog Card Number: 88-83868

Edited and designed by Kenneth R. Hine

George Booth, cartoonist

EGG-LAYING TIME, BABY!

On June 28, 1926, in Cainsville, Missouri,
there was a stirring over near Grand River.
A catfish jumped,
there was a whirlwind of dust or two,
the banks of the river caved here and there
and George Booth was born at Grandmaw's house.
Doc Duff said, "He looks like old Carp Henry . . .
got a thick short neck."

Pap and Maw Maw Booth were both schoolteachers.
Maw Maw was also a musician,
played piano, guitar, violin, French harp and sang;
she was a fine artist
winning state prizes in watercolor and oil
as well as a cartoonist.
George's training as a cartoonist
began at the age of three
when he and Maw Maw would spend
late nights together drawing funny pictures,
often until two or three in the morning.
This education was later formally supplemented
by George's not graduating
from the Corcoran School of Art in Washington, D.C.,
the Chicago Academy of Fine Arts,
the School of Visual Arts in New York City
and Adelphi College on Long Island.
Maw Maw used to say, "Stand up there, George, and
act like you know something . . .
whether you do or not!" She also told George,
"Bite off more than you can chew . . . then chew it!"

Pap was the school administrator of Fairfax;
he kept a pedagogical eye on George.
At times he considered himself a big hog man.
Pap instructed, "You can't go back and you can't stop,
so the only thing to do is go ahead."
He also said, "Jesus said,
'That unto every one which hath shall be given;
and from him that hath not, even that he hath
shall be taken away from him.'
Be ye therefore among them that hath."
Another piece of advice: "Allegiance is one thing . . .
dumb allegiance is something else."

Fairfax, Missouri, population 800, on Highway 275,
was a good place for two schoolteachers
to raise five acres of vegetables, a couple of hogs
and three boys.
The wars came, the boys went.
Pap worked as a Red Cross field director for a while.
All survived, except the hogs.
George became staff cartoonist
with *The Leatherneck*, magazine of the Marines,
in Washington, D.C.
From there he went to New York City
and looked around for six years . . .
married up, September 9, 1958, to Dione . . . Tuesday
('cause he fell in love).
One week later he accepted employment
as art director of *Tide* magazine.
After a year *Tide* was all washed up

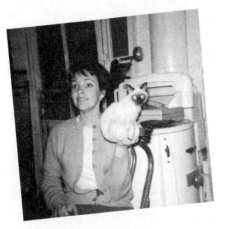

and George became corporate art director
of Bill Communications, Inc., the parent company.
He stayed on that job another seven years,
then threw a fit, quit and pursued cartooning.
He looked around another five years, until 1969,
when he began selling cartoons
to *The New Yorker* magazine.

George and Dione have one daughter, Sarah,
recently graduated from college,
and four pussycats. (The dogs are all in his head.)
A few years back Dione urged George
to rake the front yard.
George put on a stretch skirt and babushka
over beard, blue jeans and boots
to get into the mood.
A teacher from Sarah's school jogged by
with a "Good morning, Mr. Booth."
Sarah came home from school later that day
with a complaint. "It's all over school
that my dad dresses in ladies' clothes!"

This book is George's fifth published collection
of cartoons.
In addition he has done advertising, TV,
greeting cards and other books.
He also keeps busy tromping down mole runs,
stomping out grass fires
and doing diseased chicken drawings.
He hasn't raked the front yard in years.

"We are gathered here to join together this man and this woman in matrimony — a very serious step, with far-reaching and unpredictable consequences."

*"Like a duck. Calm and placid on the surface,
but paddling like hell. That's me!"*

"Mrs. Leffler says lots of men settle for the first skirt that comes along and then spend the rest of their lives regretting it. Luther, was I your first skirt?"

"Osmond! Lower your eyebrows!"

"I didn't send you a valentine."

"Everyone be home by two o'clock!"

"And whose little mole is this?"

"Ooooooh, just what I wanted!"

"Sarah's grades are excellent. She got A+ in 'Yogi Berra: Philosopher or Fall Guy?,' A in 'Dollars and Scents: An Analysis of Post-Vietnam Perfume Advertising,' A− in 'The Final Four as Last Judgment: The N.C.A.A. Tournament from a Religious Perspective,' and A in 'The American Garage Sale: Its Origins, Cultural Implications, and Future.'"

*"The Pentagon couldn't send out all those contracts and do all the im-
portant things they do every day without your grand strategy, Keatley.
Of course you have a grand strategy! Let's not hear any more of that
'I don't have a grand strategy' talk!"*

"Basil, do you think the center is going to hold?"

"You get a good suède jacket — I mean a _good_ suède jacket —
and take proper care of it, and it will last you the rest of your
natural years. You betcha!"

"Luther, I feel as if I'm waiting at a bus station."

ORDER

Buying one-color socks eliminates pairing.

Baskets of stuff stacked against the walls conserve fuel, and get the stuff out from underfoot.

For small rooms, a table hoist is a must.

Put the dishes away before you kick the dog.

Shoes can be strung.

Do not allow animals to nest.

Furniture functions better with numbers.

BOOTH.

Discipline in the home is the very linchpin of order.

"Your engine has stalled. Your engine has stalled. Carefully, now coast completely off the highway and stop. Release the hood and get out of your car. Look at your engine. Look at your engine. There are six metal-and-ceramic objects with wires attached to your engine. These are your spark plugs. These are your spark plugs. Your spark plugs are dirty, dirty, dirty. You did not release the hood. Release the hood and get out of your car. Look at your engine. Look at your engine. There are six metal-and-ceramic objects with wires attached to your engine. These are your spark plugs. These are your spark plugs. Your spark plugs are dirty, dirty, dirty."

"I've fallen in love with red paint."

"Cheery little flowers, saying good night, saying good morning!"

"Not right this second, but I'm very unhappy with that refrigerator."

"It must be snowing or sleeting someplace, because they're cancelling things in Brooklyn."

"Where in hell is today's Melon Fruit Jubilee?"

"I dreamed last night that we two-hundred-dollared Mr. Ferguson to death."

"There's lots of things in my life I absolutely needed to put in, and now there's lots of things in my life I absolutely need to get out."

"I enjoyed the sauna very much, and may I say this is the friendliest bank in my whole business experience?"

BOOTH

"The Macrocystis pyrifera of the great Pacific kelp forest is the world's fastest-growing plant. You may know it by its common name — the giant bladder kelp."

"The cat is out late tonight, but don't worry about it.
She'll come home pretty soon."

"*O.K.! So four and a half billion dollars for six hundred and eighteen guns is <u>not</u> a bargain-basement price, Keatley honey, but they most certainly <u>do</u> not need to be discussing your <u>every</u> decision in the 'Wall Street Journal' day after day after day!*"

"You have neglected to pay your bill, and Mr. Nauman,
of American Express, is livid."

"Leon, do you think that when the Cree do the Prairie-Chicken Dance they make contact with the Great Spirit?"

*"May I assume, then, that we are in agreement
on the President's 'Star Wars' proposal?"*

"My plans for the day are uncertain."

"Gigot de sept heures."

BOOTH

"Let's swap some cats today."

"Mrs. Ritterhouse charges her violin students six dollars an hour. That's two bunches of asparagus and a black-and-white cookie."

*"I don't know much about show business, but I
do know we're selling more hamburgers."*

"We have posted lower second-quarter earnings, reflecting placement of loans to Brazil, Ecuador, and Ms. Dunwoodie on non-accrual status."

"I really am very pleased with the dress I bought. It makes me feel not so dumpy and without."

"Schisgall is happy these days to forget about staying on top of the heap, and, as for me, I certainly am just as happy to let the heap do whatever it does without Schisgall on top of it all the time."

"The question, Leon, is: What is man?"

"Triple whammy."

"Let's just go in and see what happens."

"There's more inside."

"How much do you tip a masseuse?"

*"Have some more tea, Mrs. Van Sickleford. Wendell is going
to show you his mastodon tusk."*

*"How about Hardee's, Dunkin' Donuts, Holiday Inn,
H & R Block? How did <u>they</u> get started?"*

"Mrs. Beasley wants to borrow a cup of money."

"Monday, July 7, 1986. It is a quiet morning at Belle Aire. Slight fog. Beuford is fussing with his trailer hitch…"

BOOTH

"It was Saturday night. The clock on my office wall showed the time to be eleven-forty-five. There are times when a private eye does not necessarily feel like being a private eye. This was one of those times. The elevator door down the hall clanked open with a clank familiar to anyone on the fourth floor who had had an office on the fourth floor as long as I had had an office on the fourth floor. Footsteps came down the darkened hall and stopped outside my door. They were the footsteps of a woman...."

"I want two days and one dazzling night on the Orient Express!"

"I got it from Irma Shingle that the Casselberrys
are no longer living together."

"*That's Floyd Wheeler in the back of your car, Mr. Ferguson.*
He's going as far as the depot, if you would be so kind."

"Hon, I feel like riding out into big-sky country."

"_I_ thought it was delicious, but _he_ is very difficult to please."

"Don't wait up."

BOOTH

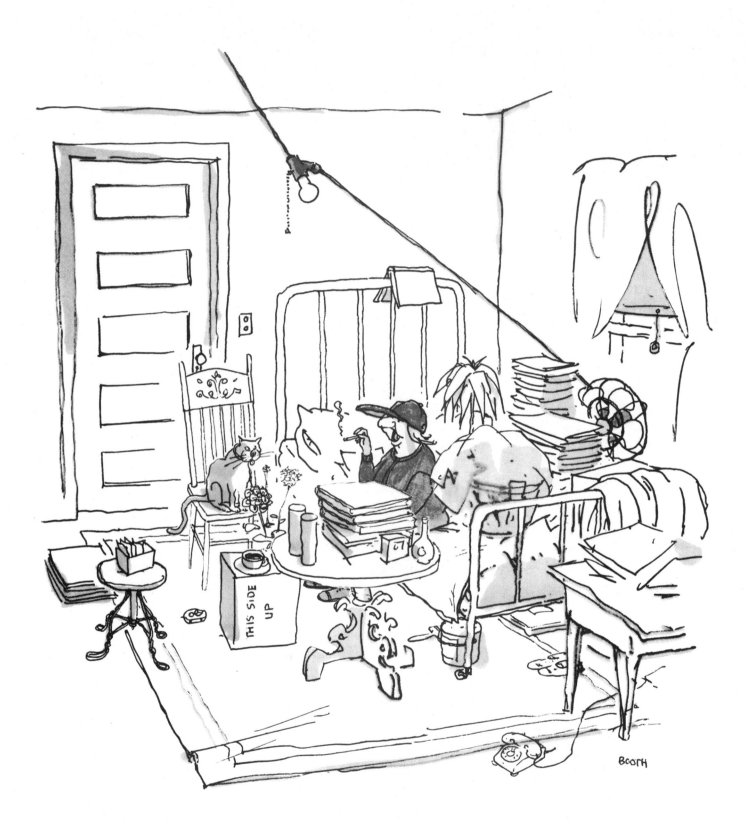

"Some of these things are just going to have to go on <u>hold</u> until Monday."

"Let me know when it's the twenty-fourth."

"Your tax return, Mr. Ferguson, for 1985 shows you want four hundred twenty-one dollars and sixty-six cents of the amount you overpaid applied to your 1986 estimated tax. However, we applied only one hundred sixty-six dollars and twenty cents to that tax, because we adjusted your account. The correction will be explained in a separate notice. Since we have not applied the full amount, you may want to: (1) correct your copy of the tax return, (2) amend your declaration of estimated tax, and (3) increase your estimated-tax payments. Otherwise, you may be charged a penalty for underpayment. No further action is required of you, Mr. Ferguson. Thank you for your cooperation."

BOOTH

"This year, tax reform has radically changed the federal tables and methods for calculating withholding taxes."

*"Here comes our first V.P., Mrs. Byers, now.
Mrs. Byers is results-oriented."*

"Please make regular coffee in the pot with brown trim and decaffeinated coffee in the pot with orange trim, so people can tell what kind it is. And do not tarry at the vaulted coffee niche."

"We see ourselves as a team. Wes may discover you have a radiator that won't make it through the summer, while Smitty may decide your transmission needs work, and at the same time Jamie just may come to the conclusion that your whole front end has been twisted out of shape."

*"Good news! She's asking for her Banana Republic
and Williams-Sonoma catalogues."*

"I don't know why everybody complains about how the Pentagon spends its money. If they had any idea how hard Keatley works to save money for everyone concerned, they would thank their lucky stars to have a man like him doing what he does in the Pentagon. Lucille, he takes those fourteen- and fifteen-year-old Vietnam airplanes, assigns them to our Air National Guard units for a while, and then eventually sells them to a little-bitty Central American ally for eight hundred thousand dollars each. That's the kind of money Keatley is saving every day. Every day, Lucille! And, of course, the little-bitty ally doesn't pay a dime of that, either, because Keatley and the Pentagon have all those details worked out in advance with the Congress."

"This is a night for white wine."

"No doubt about it. Scientifically speaking, knowledge of the river will expand in direct proportion to the length of Mr. Van Gundy's new air hose."

"*There is a Mr. Hayer at the front door with four hundred and twenty-seven legitimate ways to beat the system.*"

"Mother sends Season's Greetings with her love to you, Lydia. She says how she does so wish to spend the holidays with us but she knows that would mean we would have to drive five hundred and fifty miles to her house, as it is impossible for her to accept our invitation to come to our house, since our house, being so untidy, no offense intended, in parentheses, makes her uncomfortable to the point of actually causing her to become physically ill, but that she is willing to be a martyr all alone in order to keep everybody happy, while at the same time she is hoping with all the strength her aged bones can muster that we shall decide to drive to her house, knowing every mile of the five hundred and fifty miles that we are helping to make an old lady's heart very happy happy happy."

"I saw Harvey Yerkow today. He said, 'How's it going?' I said, 'Doing all right!'"

"Stop looking so married!"

"Each to each, I always say! Share and share alike! I take pride in my cuisine, but at the same time I am willing to divvy up household chores with a wife. Say, a wife named Irma. That is, if Irma shares as breadwinner! I'll do the cooking! We'll split the cleaning and the shopping right down the middle! Irma, you feed the dog! And help yourself to some more turnips."

"Mrs. Youttsey's Floating Island is not floating. It capsized and sank."

"What's your thinking on cracking the Pacific Rim markets?"

*"Mr. Ferguson, I want you to meet Turgut Oyleet. Turgut made
the most repairs on your car this year."*

"Stop referring to my husband as 'he whose ox is gored'!"

RETIREMENT BENEFITS

Gambol in the meadow.

Live where you want to live.

Eat breakfast every morning at The Sumptuous Plum.

You have taken enough sass in your time. Do not take any more sass.

Instead of being there for your 43-year-old daughter and her husband, go to Alaska.

Remember, at this point in time you will be forgiven almost anything.

Take another look at your will.

"War and Peace," finally.

"What happened to one o'clock?"

"The Chaetodon capistratus, commonly known as the four-eyed butterfly fish, is monogamous."

BOOTH

"Mr. Blanny has suggested that, this being almost September, and he finished late getting the storm windows in place, perhaps it would give us a chance to catch up if we skipped replacing them with the screens and go right into winter with the storm windows already in place just this one time."

*"When Bert married Mona,
he took vows for this life <u>and</u> the next."*

*"Malcolm W. Dunlap, violin repairs. Malcolm,
we are so pleased to see you."*